MW00478449

Jokes &
Riddles

For Kids of
All Ages

SWEETWATER
PRESS

Jokes & Riddles Volume 1

Copyright © 2004 Sweetwater Press

Produced by arrangement with Cliff Road Books

ISBN-13: 978-1-58173-311-2
ISBN-10: 1-58173-311-9

Book design by Pat Covert
Illustrations by Tim Rocks

Printed in the U.S.

Jokes & Riddles

For Kids of All Ages

SWEETWATER
PRESS

Jokes & Riddles

Volume 1

Q: What do you call a fairy who doesn't take a bath?

A: A Stinkerbell!

Q: Where did the king keep his armies?

A: Up his sleevies.

Q: WHAT KIND OF ILLNESS DOES BRUCE LEE GET?

A: THE KUNG FLU.

Q: Why is six scared
of seven?

A: Because 7 8 9.

Q: What do you call
a pub on Mars?

A: A mars bar.

Q: What did the teddy bear say when he was offered dessert?

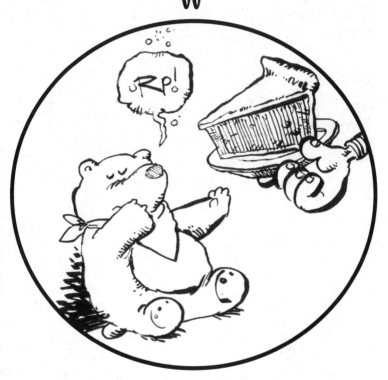

A: No thank you, I'm stuffed.

Q: WHAT IS A FIGHTER'S FAVORITE DOG?

A: A BOXER.

Q: WHAT IS A BOWLER'S FAVORITE DOG?

A: A SETTER.

Q: WHAT TOOLS DO YOU NEED IN MATH CLASS?

A: MULTI-PLIERS.

Q: What do you call a ship that lies on the bottom of the ocean and shakes?

A: A nervous wreck.

Q: What gets bigger the more you take away from it?

A: A hole.

Q: You can hear me. You can see what I do. But you cannot see me. What am I?

A: The wind.

Q: What do you call
a sheep covered in
chocolate?

A: A Hershey baaaaaaa.

Q: How deep is the
water
in a frog pond?

A: Kneedeep. Kneedeep.
Kneedeep.

Q: What did the little light bulb say to its Mom?

A: I wuv you watts and watts.

Q: What did the Pacific Ocean say to the Atlantic Ocean?

A: Nothing. It just waved.

Q: What do you call a man who doesn't sink?

A: Bob.

Q:
Why did the pony cough?

A:
He was a little hoarse.

Q: Where do aliens keep their sandwiches?

A: In a launch box.

Q: WHERE CAN YOU SEE COW ART?

A: THE MOOSEUM.

Q: What does corn wear to bed?

A: Silk.

Q:

MY MAKER NEVER
WANTS ME.
MY BUYER NEVER
USES ME.
MY USER NEVER
SEES ME.
WHAT AM I?

A:

A COFFIN.

Q: WHY DO BEES HAVE STICKY HAIR?

A: BECAUSE THEY USE A HONEY COMB.

Q: WHAT DID THE GROUND SAY TO THE EARTHQUAKE?

A: YOU CRACK ME UP.

Q: WHY DID THE ELEPHANT EAT THE CANDLE?

A: HE WANTED A LIGHT SNACK.

Q: WHAT DO YOU CALL A RODENT THAT HAS A SWORD?

A: A MOUSEKETEER.

Q: If a plane crashed on the border of England and Scotland, where would you bury the survivors?

A: You wouldn't bury the survivors.

Q: You're a bus driver. At the first stop 4 people get on. At the second stop 8 people get on, at the third stop 2 people get off, and at the fourth stop everyone gets off. What color are the bus driver's eyes?

A: The same as yours, because you ARE the bus driver.

2: What do you take before a meal?

A: A seat.

Q: Why did the chicken cross the playground?

A: To get to the other slide.

Q: David's father had three sons: Snap, Crackle, and who else?

A: David.

Q: What has a mouth but doesn't eat, a bank account but no money, a bed but doesn't sleep, and waves but has no hands?

A: A river.

Q: What do you call cheese that is not yours?

A: Nacho cheese.

Q: Why is basketball such a messy sport?

A: Because the players dribble on the floor.

Q: What is an astronaut's favorite computer key?

A: The space bar.

Q: Why are carrots good for the eyes?

A: Have you ever seen a rabbit wearing glasses?

Q: Why couldn't the skeleton go to the dance?

A: He had no body to go with.

Q: WHAT DO YOU
   CALL A FROZEN
   CAT?

A: A CATSICLE.

Q: WHAT ARE TWO
WORDS THAT DOGS
   CAN SAY?

A: BARK AND ROUGH.

Q : What is the baby motto?

A: If at first you don't succeed,
cry and cry again.

Q: What is the longest word?

A: Smile. Because there is a mile between the first and last letter.

Q: What do sheep do on a sunny day?

A: Have a baa-baa-cue.

Q: What happened when the dog swallowed a firefly?

A: It barked with de-light.

Q: WHY DO BIRDS FLY SOUTH FOR THE WINTER?

A: BECAUSE IT IS TOO FAR TO WALK.

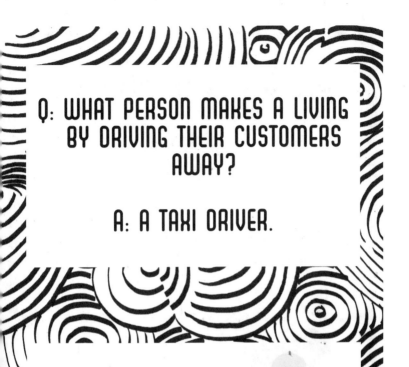

Q: WHAT PERSON MAKES A LIVING BY DRIVING THEIR CUSTOMERS AWAY?

A: A TAXI DRIVER.

Q: WHAT IS BLACK AND WHITE AND BLACK AND WHITE AND BLACK AND WHITE?

A: A ZEBRA CAUGHT IN A REVOLVING DOOR.

q: where do rabbits learn
to fly?

a: in the hare force.

q: how do you make a
milk shake?

a: give it a good scare.

q: what has four eyes but
no face?

a: mississippi.

q: why is the letter "g" so
scary?

a: it turns a host into a ghost.

Q: What did the alien say to the garden?

A: Take me to your weeder.

Q: What did the dog do with pieces of a fallen tree?

A: He barked.

Q: Why did the cook get arrested?

A: Because he beat up an egg.

Q: A man went outside in the pouring rain with no protection, but not a hair on his head got wet. Why?

A: He was bald.

Q: WHAT HAS FIVE EYES AND ONE MOUTH?

A: THE MISSISSIPPI RIVER.

Q: WHY DID THE MAN GET FIRED FROM THE M&M COMPANY?

A: BECAUSE HE THOUGHT THEY WERE ALL DEFECTIVE WITH W&W.

Q: Why did the dog chase his tail?

A: He was trying to make ends meet.

Q: What do you get when you cross a cow with a duck?

A: Milk and quackers.

Q: What letters are not
in the alphabet?

A: The ones in the mail.

Q: What did the cowboy
say when a bear ate
his dog?

A: Well doggone.

Q: WHERE DID THE PIANIST GO ON VACATION?

A: THE FLORIDA KEYS.

Q: WHAT KIND OF WORK DID THE BED DO FOR THE BLANKET?

A: UNDER COVER.

Q: Why did the golfer wear two sets of pants?

A: In case he got a hole in one.

Q: If there is a frog dead in the center of a lily pad which is right in the middle of the pond, which side would it jump to?

A: Neither, the frog is dead.

Q: What is a snake's favorite subject?

A: Hiss-tory.

Q: What do the little people drive?

A: Mini vans.

Q: What grows in size,
needs air,
but is not alive?

A: Fire.

Q: What is found on the land
and water but
does not walk or swim?

A: A snail.

44

Q: What runs but never walks and has a mouth but never talks?

A: A river.

Q: What do you call a nervous carrot?

A: An edgy veggie.

45

Q:

HOW CAN YOU
TELL THE DIFFERENCE
BETWEEN A CAN
OF CHICKEN SOUP
AND A CAN OF
TOMATO SOUP?

A:
READ THE LABEL.

Q: What did the waiter say when a customer complained that his soup tasted funny?

A: "Then why aren't you laughing?"

Q: A man was driving with no lights on and the moon was not out. A lady was crossing the street. How did he see her?

A: It was a sunny day.

Q: Why do you go to bed?

A: Because the bed won't come to you.

Q: WHAT IS THE DIFFERENCE BETWEEN CATS AND FROGS?

A: A CAT HAS NINE LIVES AND A FROG CROAKS EVERY NIGHT.

Q: WHAT IS THE DIFFERENCE BETWEEN A BUSINESS MAN AND HIS DOG?

A: A BUSINESS MAN WEARS A SUIT, HIS DOG ONLY PANTS.

Q: Why did the computer go to the doctor?

A: It had a virus.

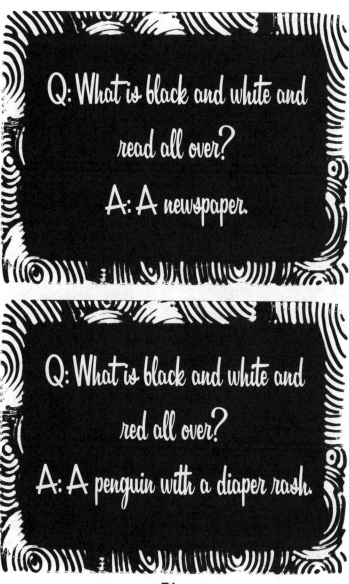

Q: What is black and white and read all over?

A: A newspaper.

Q: What is black and white and red all over?

A: A penguin with a diaper rash.

51

Q: What does a mummy call his parents?

A: Mummy and Deady.

Q: Why are astronauts so much fun?

A: Because they blast off.

Q: How do you make varnish disappear?

A: Remove the "r."

Q: Where do you learn to make ice cream?

A: Sundae school.

Q: What did the momma dog say to her puppies?

A: Hush puppies!

Q: Why was Mr. Cookie so sad?

A: He was feeling crummy.

Q: What do you call a
cow with no feet?

A: Ground beef.

Q: What do you call a
sleeping bull?

A: A bulldozer.

Q: WHY IS IT HARD TO TELL
   TWIN WITCHES APART?

A: IT IS NOT EASY TELLING
   WHICH IS WHICH.

Q: HOW DOES A BOAT
   SHOW AFFECTION?

A: IT HUGS THE SHORE.

Q:
How did the man feel when he got a big bill from the electric company?

A:
He was shocked.

Q: WHAT DO COWS DO ON SATURDAY NIGHTS?

A: GO TO THE MOO-VIES.

Q: WHY IS ENGLAND ALWAYS WET?

A: BECAUSE THE QUEEN REIGNS.

Q: What do porcupines say when they kiss?

A: Ouch!!!

Q: Why are fish so smart?

A: Because they live in schools.

Q: What did the tie say to the hat?

A: You go on a head; I'll hang around.

Q: When is a car not a car?

A: When it turns into a garage.

Q: How can you spell
eighty in two letters?

A: A-T.

Q: Did you hear the story
about the skunk?

A: Never mind. It stinks.

Q: How can you make seven even?

A: Remove the "s."

Q: How can you double your money?

A: Look at it in a mirror.

Q: Why did the atom
cross the road?

A: It was time to split.

Q: Why do Eskimos wash
their clothes
in Tide?

A: It is too cold
out-Tide.

Q: What kind of car does Luke Skywalker drive?

A: A Toy-yoda.

Q: What is the biggest pencil in the world?

A: Pennsylvania.

Q:
WHY SHOULDN'T YOU SWIM WITH A FULL STOMACH?

A:
BECAUSE IT IS MORE FUN TO SWIM WITH FRIENDS.

Q:
WHAT DO COMPUTERS
EAT FOR LUNCH?

A:
CHIPS.

Q:
WHAT RUNS BUT
NEVER WALKS?

A:
WATER.

Q: What do dogs eat at a movie theater?

A: Pupcorn.

Q: How many ears did Davy Crockett have?

A: Three: His left ear, right ear, and front-ier.

Q: What do you call two cars that collide and twitch?

A: A nervous wreck.

Q: What did the pickle say when he got to the card game?

A: Dill me in.

Q: Where do you find
a no-legged dog?

A: Right where you
left him.

Q: Why do bagpipers
walk when they play?

A: They're trying to get
away from the noise.

How do you prevent a summer cold?

Catch it in the winter.

What is the best day of the week to sleep?

A snooze day.

Q: Were you long in the hospital?

A: No, I was the same size I am now.

Q:

What did the jailbird say to the Texas judge?

A:

Howdy Pardoner!

Q: Why did the actor fall through the floor?

A: It was just a stage he was going through.

Q: What did the mayonnaise say when the refrigerator door opened?

A: Close the door! I'm dressing!

Q: What stories do the ship captain's children like to hear?

A: Ferry tales.

Q: What kind of car does Mickey Mouse's wife drive?

A: A Minnie van.

Q: Why was the broom late?

A: It over swept.

Q: What kind of hair do oceans have?

A: Wavy.

Q: Why did the turkey cross the road?

A: It was the chicken's day off.

Q: What do pigs put on cuts?

A: Oink-ment.

Q: Why do fish live in salt water?

A: Because pepper makes them sneeze.

Q: Why did the snowman call his dog Frost?

A: Because frost bites.

Q: What game do cows play at parties?

A: Moosical chairs.

Q: HOW DO YOU MAKE A LEMON DROP?

A: HOLD IT THEN LET GO.

Q: WHY DID THE MUDDY CHICKEN CROSS THE ROAD AND COME BACK AGAIN?

A: BECAUSE HE WAS A DIRTY DOUBLE CROSSER.

Q: WHAT DID THE DOG SAY WHEN HE SAW TWO WOLVES?

A: WOOF! WOOF!

Q: HOW CAN YOU NAME THE CAPITAL OF EVERY US STATE IN TWO SECONDS?

A: WASHINGTON, DC.

KNOCK, KNOCK!

WHO'S THERE?

EARL.

EARL WHO?

EARL BE GLAD TO TELL YOU WHEN YOU OPEN THE DOOR!

KNOCK, KNOCK!

WHO'S THERE?

BOO.

BOO WHO?

DON'T CRY. IT'S ONLY A JOKE.

Knock, knock!

Who's there?

Emma.

Emma who?

Emma bit cold out here. Will you let me in?

Knock, knock!

Who's there?

Howl.

Howl who?

Howl you know unless you open the door?

Knock, knock!
Who's there?
Cows.
Cows who?
Cows don't who.
They moo.

Knock, knock!
Who's there?
Duey.
Duey who?
Duey have to keep telling
Knock, knock jokes?

Knock, knock!
Who's there?
Cargo.

Cargo who?
Cargo beep beep.

Q: What did the frog order at McDonald's?

A: French flies and a diet Croak.

Q: Why did the frog say meow?

A: Because he was learning another language.

Knock, knock!

Who's there?

Little old lady.

Little old lady who?

I didn't know you could yodel!

Knock, knock!
Who's there?
Thor.
Thor who?
Thor loser, aren't you?

Knock, knock!
Who's there?
Noah.
Noah who?
Noah about building
an ark?

Q: WHAT DO BABY GHOSTS DRINK?

A: EVAPORATED MILK.

Q: WHEN DO GHOSTS USUALLY APPEAR?

A: JUST BEFORE SOMEONE SCREAMS.

Q: WHAT DO YOU GET IF BATMAN AND ROBIN GET SMASHED BY A STEAM ROLLER?

A: FLATMAN AND RIBBON.

2: What gets harder to catch the faster you run?

A: Your breath.

2: What never gets wetter no matter how much it rains?

A: The sea.

2: What would you find
on a cursed beach?

A: A Sand-witch.

2: What did the policeman
say when the spider
ran down his back?

A: You're under a vest!

Q: Why did the king go to the dentist?

A: To get his teeth crowned.

Q: Who tells people where to get off for a living?

A: A bus driver.

Q: What should you say when you meet a ghost?

A: How do you boo?

Q: What kind of bus can cross the ocean?

A: Colum-bus.

Q: What kind of sandwich speaks for itself?

A: A tongue sandwich.

Q: Which baseball player serves lemonade?

A: The pitcher.

Q: Why did the cucumber hire a lawyer?

A: He was in a pickle.

Q: What is the difference between a nail and a boxer?

A: One gets knocked in while the other gets knocked out.

Q: What did the little ghost order at the Italian restaurant?

A: Spook-ghetti!

Q: Do you want to hear a dirty joke?

A: A pig jumped in the mud.

Q: Why did the pitcher let the batter walk?

A: He was too tired to run.

Q: What did the surgeon say to the patient when the operation was over?

A: That's enough out of you.

Q: Why did the child study in the airplane?

A: He wanted a higher education.

Q: Who tells jokes about knitting?

A: A knit wit.

Q: What do you call two strawberries having a meeting?

A: A strawberry shake.

Q: What billiard
game is
played in the water?

A: Swimming pool.

Q: What can a whole
orange do that a half
orange can't?

A: Look round.

Q: What do you give a horse with a cold?

A: Cough stirrup.

Q: What does a lion eat
when he goes to a
restaurant?

A: The waiter.

Q: What goes out black
and comes in white?

A: A black cow in a
snow storm.

Q: What do giants tell in their spare time?

A: Tall tales.

Q: What do you call a piece of wood with nothing to do?

A: Board.

Q: What do you get when
peas fight?

A: Black-eyed peas.

Q: What did one car muffler
say to the other car muffler?

A: I am exhausted.

Q:

Which planet is most suitable for long distance calls?

A:

Saturn, because it has so many rings.

Q: How does the moon cut his hair?

A: Eclipse it!

Q: WHAT KIND OF CHEESE DO YOU USE TO BUILD A HOUSE?

A: COTTAGE CHEESE.

Q: WHAT HAPPENED TO THE PLANT IN THE MATH CLASSROOM?

A: IT GREW SQUARE ROOTS.

Q: WHERE DID THE SHEEP GET A HAIR CUT?

A: AT THE BAA-BER SHOP.

Q: WHERE DOES A CRIMINAL WITH A SWEET TOOTH BELONG?

A: BEHIND CHOCOLATE BARS.

Q. WHAT DO YOU CALL
A RABBIT THAT TELLS
JOKES?

A. A FUNNY BUNNY.

Q. WHAT DO YOU CALL
A CAT THAT TELLS
JOKES?

A. A WITTY KITTY.

Q. WHAT DO YOU CALL IT WHEN IT RAINS CHICKENS AND DUCKS?

A: FOWL WEATHER.

Q: What do you call
a female friend?

A: A gal pal.

Q: What do you call
a funny goat?

A: A silly billy.

Q:What do you call
a platter of worms?

A:A bait plate.

Q: How does a flea
make a cake?

A: From scratch.

Q: WHAT DO DOGS PUT ON THEIR PIZZA?

A: MUTTS-ARELLA.

Q: HOW LONG SHOULD DOCTORS PRACTICE MEDICINE?

A: UNTIL THEY GET IT RIGHT.

Q: WHAT DO YOU CALL TWO RACERS WHO DRIVE THE SAME CAR?

A: VROOM-MATES.

Q: What is a boxer's favorite drink?

A: Fruit punch.

Q: How do you get a one-handed blonde out of a tree?

A: Wave to her.

Q: What did the rope say to the scissors?

A: Cut me some slack!

Q: Why are graveyards so noisy?

A: Because of all the coffin.

Q: What did the ocean say to the other ocean?

A: Long time no see.

Q: What did one elevator say to the other elevator?

A: I think I'm coming down with something.

Q: What do you say to a hitchhiking frog?

A: Hop in!

Q: When is the moon heaviest?

A: When it is full.

Q: What's in your pocket when it is empty?

A: A hole.

Q: How do bears walk in the woods?

A: With their bear feet.

Q: What do policemen eat at the movies?

A: Cop-corn.

Q: Why do ranchers ride their horses?

A: Because they are too heavy to carry.

Q: WHAT IS A COW'S FAVORITE SOUP?

A: MOO STEW.

Q: WHAT DO YOU CALL AN ANGRY BOY?

A: A MAD LAD.

Q: WHAT IS IN THE MIDDLE OF EARTH?

A: THE LETTER "R."

Q: WHAT HAPPENED TO THE CAT WHO ATE WOOL?

A: SHE HAD MITTENS.

Q: HOW MUCH DOES
   A POUND OF
   BUTTER WEIGH?

A: A POUND.

Q: WHY WAS TIGGER
   LOOKING IN THE
   TOILET?

A: HE WAS LOOKING
   FOR POOH.

Q: WHAT IS THE MOST INTELLIGENT ARTICLE OF CLOTHING?

A: SMARTY PANTS.

Q: WHAT DO YOU GET WHEN YOU CROSS LASSIE WITH A TULIP?

A: A COLLIE-FLOWER.

Q: WHAT DO YOU DO IF a BULL CHARGES YOU?

a: YOU PAY HIM.

Q: What is the
friendliest animal?
A: A Hi-ena.

Q: What part of your eye
goes to school?

A: The pupil.

Q: What position does the dry cleaner play?

A: Shirt stop.

Q: What did the hair say to the hairdresser?

A: Do Not tease me!

Q: Who is the best fencer in the ocean?

A: A sword fish.

Q:

WHAT DID ONE GERM SAY TO THE OTHER GERM?

A:

YOU ARE MAKING ME SICK.

Q:

WHY DID THE PAINTER GO TO JAIL?

A:

BECAUSE HE HAD A BRUSH WITH THE LAW.

Q: Why didn't the pirate play cards?

A: Because he was sitting on the deck.

Q: What do you do with a tissue that won't dance?

A: You put a little boogie in it.

Q: How do you ride
a horse
with no legs?

A: You don't. It has
no legs.

Q: Why was George
Washington buried
standing up?

A: Because he
never lied.

Q: WHY DID THE HOTEL HIRE THE FROG?

A: THEY NEEDED A BELL HOP.

Q: WHO TELLS PEOPLE WHERE TO GO AND GETS AWAY WITH IT?

A: A TRAVEL AGENT.

Q: Why was the waiter good at tennis?

A: He practiced serving.

Q: What makes the road broad?

A: The letter "b."

Q: How do you make fruit punch?

A: You give it boxing lessons.

Q: Where do judges go for fun?

A: Tennis court.

Q: When will a mathematician die?

A: When his number is up.

Q: Why did the scientist install a knocker on his door?

A: He wanted to win the no-bell prize.

Q: What kind of tracks does the King leave in the sand?

A: Foot prince.

Q: How do you call a dog with no legs?

A: You don't. It won't come anyway.

Q: Why did the toilet always win at cards?

A: It always had a flush.

Q: What did the envelope say to the stamp?

A: Stick with me and we'll go places.

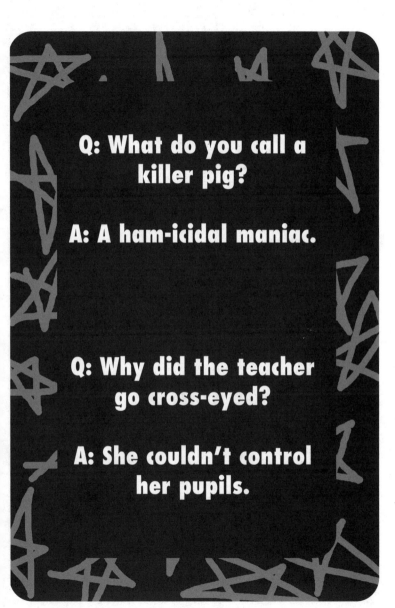

Q: What do you call a killer pig?

A: A ham-icidal maniac.

Q: Why did the teacher go cross-eyed?

A: She couldn't control her pupils.

Q: How does the IRS agent get around town?

A: Tax-is.

Q: What kind of car do you drive in the fall?

A: An autumn-mobile.

Q: What sits by your bed at night with its tongue sticking out?

A: Your shoe.

Q: Who rides in funny looking cars?

A: Car-toonists.

Q: What color hair do most witches have?

A: Brew-nette.

Q: What kind of gum do hens chew?

A: Chick-lets.

Q: What kind of eyeglasses do spies wear?

A: Spy-focals.

Q: Why were the ducks worried?

A: Because they had so many bills.

Q: What is the favorite dessert
of cartoons?

A: Mickey Mousse.

Q: What do you call a mouse
that bathes every day?

A: Squeaky clean.

Q: WHAT DO YOU CALL
A CAR THAT BREAKS DOWN?

A: A CAB.

Q: WHAT GOES AROUND
THE WORLD BUT STAYS
IN THE SAME SPOT?

A: A STAMP.

Q: WHAT IS A CAT'S FAVORITE COLOR?

A: PURR-PLE.

Q: WHY DID THE PIANO NOT SHOW UP TO WORK?

A: BECAUSE IT LOST ITS KEYS.

Q: What kind of fish
works at a hospital?

A: A sturgeon.

Q: What is necessary
clothing for Wall Street
workers?

A: Stockings.

Q: Where do dinosaurs vacation?

A: At the dino-shore.

Q: What grows down
when it grows up?

A: A goose.

Q: What is up and
never comes down?

A: The sky.

Q: Where do baby trees go to school?

A: The nursery.

Q: How do you encourage an egg?

A: You egg it on.

Q: SIX KIDS AND TWO DOGS WERE WALKING UNDER ONE UMBRELLA. HOW COME THEY DID NOT GET WET?

A: IT WAS NOT RAINING.

Q: WHAT IS THE BEST
   KIND OF MAIL
   ON A HOT DAY?

A: FAN MAIL

Q: WHAT DO YOU CALL
A FISH THAT WILL NOT
      SHARE?

A: SHELLFISH.

Q: WHY DO VAMPIRES LIKE ART CLASS THE BEST?

A: BECAUSE THEY LIKE TO DRAW BLOOD.

q: what occurs once in a minute,
twice in a moment,
and never in a thousand years?

a: the letter "m."

q: how can a cowboy ride in to
town on friday, stay four
nights, and ride out on friday?

a: his horse is named friday.

Q: WHICH IS CORRECT:
THE YOLK OF AN EGG
IS WHITE OR
THE YOLK OF AN
EGG ARE WHITE?

A: NEITHER.
THE YOLK OF AN EGG
IS YELLOW.

Q: THERE IS A ONE-STORY HOUSE IN WHICH EVERYTHING IS PINK. WHAT COLOR ARE THE STAIRS?

A: THERE ARE NO STAIRS. IT'S A ONE-STORY HOUSE.

2: What do moths study in school?

A: Moth-ematics.

2: What is so fragile that saying its name can break it?

A: Silence.

Q: What can you put in a wooden box to make it lighter?

A: Holes.

Q: Where do frogs keep their money?

A: In the river bank.

Q: What do you call a blind deer?

A: No eye deer.

Q: Why did the blonde take a ruler to bed?

A: She wanted to see how long she slept.

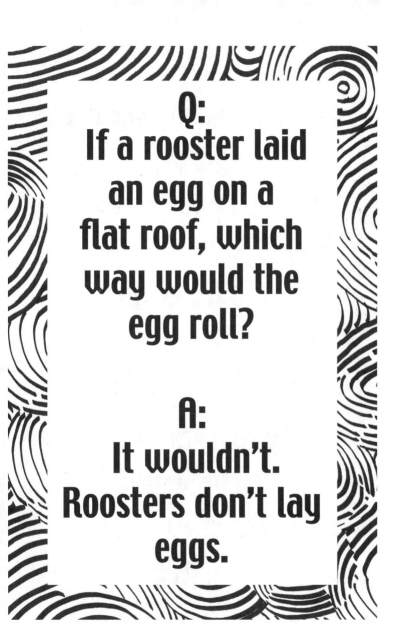

Q:
If a rooster laid an egg on a flat roof, which way would the egg roll?

A:
It wouldn't. Roosters don't lay eggs.

**Q: What kind of bone keeps getting
longer and shorter?**

A: A trombone.

**Q: If you drop a yellow hat
in the Red Sea what does
it become?**

A: Wet.

Q: What goes up but never goes down?

A: Your age.

Q: What do you get when you cross a parrot with a tiger?

A: I don't know, but you better listen carefully.

Q: What seven letters did old Mother Hubbard say when she opened her cupboard?

A: O-I-C-U-R-M-T.

Q: WHAT ENGLISH WORD DOES EVERYONE PRONOUNCE INCORRECTLY?

A: INCORRECTLY.

Q: WHAT DO YOU CALL YOUR FATHER-IN-LAW'S ONLY CHILD'S MOTHER-IN-LAW?

A: MOM.

Q:
IF YOU HAVE THREE APPLES AND THREE ORANGES IN ONE HAND AND THREE APPLES AND THREE ORANGES IN THE OTHER, WHAT DO YOU HAVE?

A:
REALLY BIG HANDS.

Q: Imagine you are in a room with no doors or windows. How do you get out?

A: Stop imagining.

Q: If you were locked in a car with a hammer, what would you do?

A: Unlock the door.

Q: The farmer had 18 cows. They all died but 9. How many cows does he have?

A: Nine.

Why did they cross the road jokes!

Q: Why did the turtle cross the road?

A: To get to the shell station.

Q: Why did the starfish cross the road?

A: To get to the other tide.

Q: Why did the fox cross the road?

A: To get the chicken.

Q: Why did the turkey cross the road twice?

A: To prove it was not chicken.

Q: WHY DO LIONS EAT RAW MEAT?

A: BECAUSE THEY NEVER LEARNED HOW TO COOK.

Q: WHY DON'T THE ZEBRAS PLAY GAMES?

A: THERE ARE TOO MANY CHEETAHS.

Q: HOW MANY ANIMALS DID MOSES TAKE ON THE ARK?

A: NONE, IT WAS NOAH.

Q: WHY DO CHICKENS LAY EGGS?

A: BECAUSE IF THEY DROPPED THEM THEY WOULD BREAK.

Q:What goes ha-ha plop?

A: Someone laughing his head off!

Q: When can you put pickles in a door?

A: When it's ajar.

Q: What do you call a song about a car?

A: A car tune.

Q: Why did the rabbit go to the barber?

A: To get a hare cut.

Q: How much is the cheapest perfume?

A: A scent.

Q: What are the most delicious books?

A: Cookbooks.

Q: Where's the best place to see a monster?

A: From far away.

Q: Why did the policeman go to the baseball game?

A: He wanted to catch the players stealing bases.

Q: Why did the lamp
flunk all his classes?

A: It wasn't very bright.

Q: What do you
find in a clean nose?

A: Fingerprints.

Q: What is a bully's favorite food?

A: A knuckle sandwich.

Q: What time does a rocket get hungry?

A: At launch time.

Q: What does a spider order for lunch?

A: Hamburger and flies.

Q: Why didn't the pirate go to the movie?

A: It was rated rrrrrrr.

Q: WHY HAS NO ONE SPOTTED A LEOPARD IN AFRICA?

A: BECAUSE LEOPARDS ARE ALREADY SPOTTED.

Q: A BUTCHER IS SIX FEET TALL, WEARS A SIZE FOURTEEN SHOE, AND HAS A FIFTY INCH WAIST. WHAT DOES HE WEIGH?

A: MEAT.

Q: Why did Cinderella's soccer team always lose?

A: Because her coach was a pumpkin.

Q: What is a skunk worth?

A: One scent.

Q: What is the largest ant in the world?

A: Antarctica.

Q: What kind of monkey can fly?

A: A hot air baboon.

Q: What did the sock say to the foot?

A: You're putting me on.

Q: Why did Mickey Mouse go to space?

A: He wanted to go see Pluto.

Q: If there are three apples and you take away two, how many do you have?

A: Two.

Q: What kind of
facial hair does a
cow have?

A: A mooooo-stache.

Q: Why did the blonde
nurse take a red magic
marker to work?

A: In case she had to
draw blood.

Q: How do rabbits travel?

A: By hare-o-plane.

Q: What did the banana
do when it heard
the ice cream?

A: It split.

Q: Why can't bikes stand
up by themselves?

A: Because they are
two-tired.

Q: Why did the blonde get excited when she finished the puzzle in six months?

A: Because the box said 2-4 years.

Q: What do you call a pampered cow?

A: Spoiled milk.

Q: What do you get when you cross a snowman with a vampire?

A: Frostbite.

Q: What has a
tongue
but cannot talk?

A: A shoe.

Q: What can fill up
a room but
takes up no space?

A: Light.

Q: What has three feet but cannot walk?

A: A yard.

Q: What has a head and tail but has no legs?

A: A penny.

Q:

THE BEGINNING OF
ETERNITY,
THE END OF SPACE,
THE BEGINNING OF
EVERY END,
THE END OF EVERY
PLACE.

WHAT AM I?

A:

THE LETTER E.

Q: What do whales like to chew?

A: Blubber gum.

Q: Can giraffes have babies?

A: No, only giraffes.

Q: What should you wear if your basement is flooded?

A: Pumps.

Q: What kind of clothing does a house wear?

A: Address.

Q: What kind of ties can you not wear?

A: Railroad ties.

Q: What is light as a feather but cannot be held very long?

A: Your breath.

Q: What is the best time to eat breakfast?

A: When you get up in the morning.

Q: What kind of storm is always in a rush?

A: A hurry-cane.

Q: Thin I am quick, fat I am slow, the wind is my foe. What am I?

A: A candle, of course!

Q:What did one potato chip say to the other potato chip?

A:Wanna go for a dip?

Q: Why did the gum cross the road?

A: It was stuck to the chicken's foot.

Q: Why did the skeleton refuse to cross the road?

A: It didn't have any guts.

Q: What do skunks put in their shoes?

A: odor eaters.

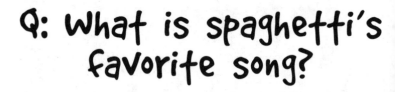

Q: What is spaghetti's favorite song?

A: Yankee Noodle

Q: What paper is most likely to sneeze?

A: A tissue.

Q: Where do ducks get their vocabulary?

A: The duck-tionary.

Q: Why did the pauper become a baker?

A: He kneaded the dough.

Q: What comes after "I seven the house"?

A: I eight the house.

Q: What fruit do ghosts like best?

A: Boo-berries.

Q: What do sea dragons eat for dinner?

A: Fish and ships.

Q: WHY IS THE SUN SO BRIGHT?

A: BECAUSE IT PAID ATTENTION IN CLASS.

Q: WHAT STARTS WITH P, ENDS WITH E, AND HAS A THOUSAND LETTERS IN IT?

A: THE POST OFFICE.

Q: How does a king open a door?

A: With a monarchy.

q: what do you call a funny book about eggs?

a: a yolk book.

q: why are potatoes good detectives?

a: because they keep their eyes peeled.

q: why was the belt arrested?

a: for holding up the pants.

q: forwards it is heavy, backwards it is not. what is it?

a: a ton.

Q: Why did the woman wear a hard hat to the dinner table?

A: She was on a crash diet.

Q: What do you get
when you cut a comedian
in two?

A: A half wit.

Q: When is it dangerous
to play cards?

A: When the joker is wild.

Q: WHAT HAS FOUR WHEELS AND FLIES?

A: A GARBAGE TRUCK.

Q: WHAT DO SKELETONS SAY BEFORE EATING?

A: BONE APPETITE!

Q: WHAT IS A BULL BEFORE HE GROWS UP?

A: A COW BOY.

Q: WHY WON'T AN OYSTER SHARE HIS TOYS?

A: BECAUSE HE IS SHELLFISH.

Q: WHAT KIND OF SODA
IS BAD TO DRINK?

A: BAKING SODA.

Q: WHY DID THE CAKE
LIKE TO PLAY BASEBALL?

A: BECAUSE IT WAS A
GOOD BATTER.

Q: WHY DIDN'T THE HOTDOG STAR IN THE MOVIES?

A: BECAUSE THE ROLLS WEREN'T GOOD ENOUGH.

Q: WHERE IS THE OCEAN THE DEEPEST?

A: ON THE BOTTOM.

Q: WHAT DID THE BEACH SAY WHEN THE TIDE CAME IN?

A: LONG TIME NO SEA.

Q: WHAT DOES MOTHER EARTH USE TO FISH?

A: NORTH AND SOUTH POLES.

Q: WHERE IS THE BEST PLACE TO SEE FISH?

A: IN A SEAFOOD RESTAURANT.

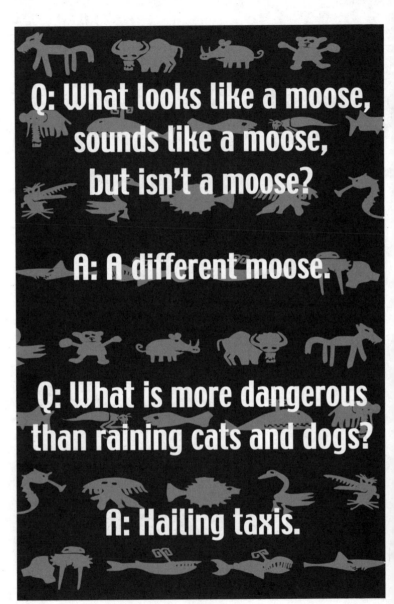

Q: What looks like a moose,
sounds like a moose,
but isn't a moose?

A: A different moose.

Q: What is more dangerous
than raining cats and dogs?

A: Hailing taxis.

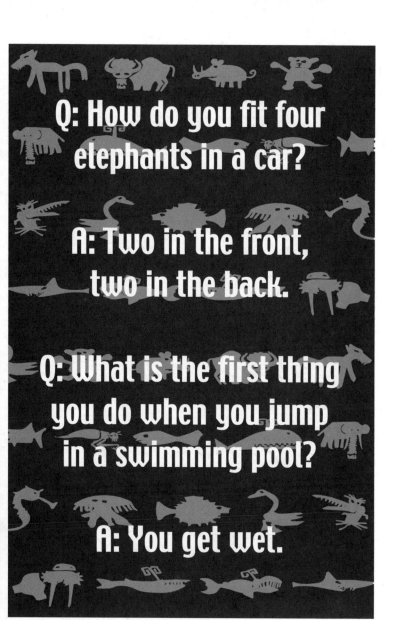

Q: How do you fit four elephants in a car?

A: Two in the front, two in the back.

Q: What is the first thing you do when you jump in a swimming pool?

A: You get wet.

Q: What part of your body has the most rhythm?

A: Your eardrums.

Q: What is a pickle's all-time favorite musical?

A: Hello, Dilly!

Q: What is a cannibal's favorite game?

A: Swallow the leader.

Q: WHAT IS USEFUL
WHEN IT IS BROKEN?

A: AN EGG.

Q: WHERE DO ONE-EYED
MONSTERS LOOK UP
INFORMATION?

A: THE EN-CYCLOPS-PEDIA.

Q: What did one spoon say to the other?

A: Let's stir things up.

Q: Where do animals get prescriptions filled?

A: Old Mac Donald's Farm-acy.

Q: What did the chocolate bar say to the lollipop?

A: Hello, sucker.

Q: What did one mountain say to the other mountain?

A: Meet me in the valley.

Q: What is black and white and pink all over?

A: An embarrassed zebra.

Q: What do you need when you spot an iceberg 20 miles away?

A: I dunno, but you don't need glasses.

Q: WHY IS DRACULA SO UNPOPULAR?

A: HE IS A PAIN IN THE NECK.

Q: WHAT BIRD STEALS FROM THE RICH TO GIVE TO THE POOR?

A: ROBIN HOOD.

Q: WHAT DID THE TOILET SAY TO THE OTHER TOILET?

A: YOU LOOK A LITTLE FLUSHED.

Q: What happens when ducks fly upside-down?

A: They quack up.

Q: What is less than an inch from your eyes but you can never see it?

A: Your forehead.

Q: What does an elephant do just before he leaves town?

A: He packs his trunk.

Q: How does a frog tell you to get a stain out?

A: Rub it. Rub it.

Q: If you are an American outside the bathroom, what are you inside the bathroom?

A: European.

Q: How do you change a pumpkin into another vegetable?

A: You throw it in the air and it comes down a squash.

Q: IF TWO'S COMPANY AND
THREE'S A CROWD,
WHAT ARE FOUR AND FIVE?

A: NINE.

Q: WHAT TIME IS IT WHEN
AN ELEPHANT SITS ON
A FENCE?

A: TIME TO GET A NEW FENCE.

Q: THE MORE YOU TAKE THE
MORE YOU LEAVE BEHIND.
WHAT IS IT?

A: FOOTSTEPS.

Q: HAVE YOU HEARD ABOUT
THE NEW RESTAURANT ON
THE MOON?

A: GREAT FOOD, BUT NO ATMOSPHERE.

Q: Who steals the soap in the bathroom?

A: The robber duckie.

Q: WHAT DO YOU CALL A LAMB ATTACK SHIP?

A: BATTLESHEEP.

Q: IF YOU TAKE OFF MY SKIN I WILL NOT CRY BUT YOU WILL. WHAT AM I?

A: AN ONION.

Q: What is Smoky the Bear's middle name?

A: The.

Q: What always runs and never walks, tells you something but never talks?

A: A clock.

Q: Who goes with three before her and five behind?

A: Four.

Q: Why do witches fly on brooms?

A: Vacuum cleaner cords aren't long enough.

2: *All about the house, with his lady he dances. Yet he always works and never romances. What is he?*

A: A broom.

Q: I WAS CARRIED INTO A DARK ROOM AND SET ON FIRE. I WEPT. WHAT AM I?

A: A CANDLE.

Q: WHAT FLOATS ON WATER AS LIGHT AS A FEATHER YET A THOUSAND MEN CAN'T LIFT IT?

A: A BUBBLE.

Q: What has four legs but can't walk?

A: A table.

Q: What kind of house weighs the least?

A: A lighthouse.

Q: What is always coming but never arrives?

A: Tomorrow.

Q: When does Friday come before Thursday?

A: In the dictionary.

Q: WHAT KIND OF MISTAKES
DO SPOOKS MAKE?

A: BOO BOOS.

Q: WHAT DO YOU CALL
A SKELETON THAT WON'T
WORK?

A: LAZY BONES.

Q: WHAT DO WITCHES PUT
ON THEIR HAIR IN THE
MORNING?

A: SCARE SPRAY.

Q: WHEN IS IT BAD LUCK
TO MEET A BLACK CAT?

A: WHEN YOU ARE A MOUSE.

Q: What goes to bed with his shoes on?

A: A horse.

Q: What do you call a scared dinosaur?

A: A nervous rex.

Q: What did the spider do on the computer?

A: He made a web site.

Q: What is a quick way to double your money?

A: You fold it.

Q: How did Ben Franklin discover electricity?

A: It came to him in a flash.

Q: What did one wall say
   to the other wall?

A: Meet you at the corner.

Q: What do you get
when you cross two
banana peels?

A: A pair of slippers.

Q: The more you have
it the less you see.
What is it?

A: Darkness.

Q: By moon or sun I can
be found, but if there is
no light I am not around.
What am I?

A: A shadow.

Q: Why did the man throw his clock out the window?

A: To see time fly.

q: it can bring back
the dead;
make us cry,
make us laugh,
make us young;
yet lasts a lifetime?
what is it?

a: a memory.

q: you use it between
your hands,
your fingers,
and your toes,
the more it works
the thinner it grows.
what is it?

a: a bar of soap.

Q: Why do mummies make good employees?

A: They get all wrapped up in their work.

Q: What happened when 500 hares got loose in the street?

A: The policeman had to comb the area.

Q: Why does it get so hot after a baseball game?

A: Because all the fans leave.

Q: What word begins with the letter "t," ends in the letter "t," and is filled with tea?

A: A teapot.

Q: WHY DID THE BOY EAT HIS HOMEWORK?

A: BECAUSE THE TEACHER SAID IT WAS A PIECE OF CAKE.

Q: Why doesn't tuna
slide
off your plate?

A: Because fish sticks.

Q: How can you catch
a school of fish?

A: With a bookworm.

Q: What does a bird need when it is sick?

A: Tweet-ment.

Q: Did you hear the joke about the butter?

A: Better not spread it!

Q: What is the difference between here and there?

A: The letter "t."

Q: How do you know peanuts are fattening?

A: Ever see a skinny elephant?

Q: What is the richest kind of air?

A: A millionaire.

Q: Why is it that everyone loves Michael the Mushroom?

A: Because he is such a fungi.

Q: What do you call a cheese that is not yours?

A: Mine.

Q: Who is strong enough to move a castle?

A: Any chess player.

Q: What day do
fish
hate the most?

A: Fry-day.

Q: How do you
catch a
unique rabbit?

A: Unique up on
him.

Q: How do you
catch
a tame rabbit?

A: The tame way.

Q: Is your
refrigerator
running?

A: Better go
catch it!

Q:

WHAT IS PRONOUNCED
LIKE ONE LETTER,
WRITTEN IN THREE
LETTERS, AND BELONGS
TO ALL ANIMALS?

A: EYE.

Q:

IF YOU HAVE IT, YOU
WANT TO SHARE IT.
IF YOU SHARE IT, YOU
DON'T HAVE IT. WHAT IS IT?

A: A SECRET.

Q: WHAT ALWAYS SMELLS BUT HAS NO ODOR?

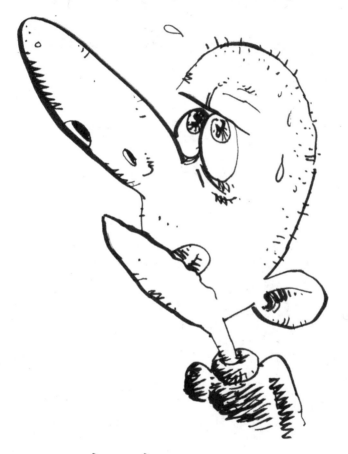

A: A NOSE.

Q: WHAT DO YOU ADD
TO OIL TO MAKE IT BOIL?

A: YOU ADD THE
LETTER "B."

Q: DID YOU HEAR ABOUT
THE FIGHT AT THE FISH
CAMP LAST NIGHT?

A: TWO FISH GOT BATTERED.

Q: WHERE DID THE FORTUNE TELLER GO ON HER VACATION?

A: PALM BEACH.

Q: WHY DID SILLY BILLY SIT ON THE CLOCK?

A: BECAUSE HE WANTED TO BE ON TIME.

Q: WHAT DO YOU CALL A FRIENDLY DEAD EGYPTIAN?

A: A CHUMMY MUMMY.

Q: WHAT STREETS DO GHOSTS HAUNT?

A: DEAD ENDS.

Q: WHAT TESTS DO ALL YOUNG WITCHES HAVE TO PASS?

A: A SPELL-ING TEST.

Q: What makes
a chess
player happy?

A: Taking a knight off.

Q: What turns everything
around but does not
move?

A: A mirror.

Q: What is the easiest
thing to part with?

A: A comb.

Q: Why did the
baker
stop making donuts?

A: He got tired of the
hole business.

Q: If you had only one match and entered a room with an oil lamp, kerosene lamp, a candle, and a wood stove, which would you light first?

A: The match.

Q: What do you get
when you cross a
dinosaur
with a dog?

A: A very nervous mailman.

Q: Before Mt. Everest
was discovered,
what mountain was
the tallest on Earth?

A: Mt. Everest.

Q: Which travels faster: heat or cold?

A: Heat. You can catch a cold.

Q: Where can you find roads without cars, forests without trees, and cities without houses?

A: A map.

Q: Why did the cowboy
buy a dachshund?

A: He wanted to get
a long little doggie.

Q: There is an ancient
invention still used today
that allows people to see
through walls. What is it?

A: A window.

Q: What do you call a girl with a frog on her head?

A: Lily.

Q: What is a frog's favorite drink?

A: Croak-a-cola.

RIBBET, RIBBET!

Q: How do frogs march in the army?

A: Hop two three four!

Q: I am asleep by day
and fly by night.
I have no feathers
to aid my flight.
What am I?

A: A bat.

Q: What do you call a man with a seagull on his head?

A: cliff.

Q: What kind of flower does everyone have?

A: Tulips.

Q: What did one eye say to the other eye?

A: There's something between us that smells.

Q: Why did Alex keep his guitar in the refrigerator?

A: Because he liked to play cool music.

Q: What did the polite mouse say?

A: Cheese and thank you.

Q:
What is in the
middle of the sea?

A:
The letter "e."

Q:
When is a piece of
wood like a king?

A:
When it is a ruler.

Q:
Which rope could
you never skip with?

A:
Europe.

Q:
Did you hear the
story about the wall?

A:
You'll never get over it!

Q : What has eyes and no nose, a tongue but no teeth, and is a foot long?

A: A boot.

Q : What is worse than finding a worm in your apple?

A: Finding only half the worm.

Q: Why was Thomas Edison able to invent the light bulb?

A: Because he was very bright.

Q: What did one strawberry say to the other?

A: If you weren't so sweet we wouldn't be in this jam.

Q: WHAT IS A GHOUL'S FAVORITE FOOD?

A: GHOULASH.

Q: HOW DOES A VAMPIRE ORDER HIS COFFEE?

A: DE-COFFIN-ATED.